In Spite of
Everything...

In Spite of Everything...

A Book of Poems

Curtis Robbins

In Spite of Everything...
A Book of Poems

iUniverse books may be ordered through booksellers or by contacting:

iUniverse
1663 Liberty Drive
Bloomington, IN 47403
www.iuniverse.com
844-349-9409

ISBN: 978-1-4917-6155-7 (sc)
ISBN: 978-1-4917-6156-4 (e)

Library of Congress Control Number: 2015902889

Print information available on the last page.

iUniverse rev. date: 08/22/2023

For my wife, Susan, and
our children, Benjamin and Rebecca

Contents

Acknowledgments

"Comparison," "Persona Non Gratis," and "They Call Me by the Labels" in *The Tactile Mind Quarterly* (Summer 2004), J. L. Clark, editor.

"Solo Dining While Growing Up," "No Rhythm, They Say," "Empty Ears," and "The Promised World" in *The Deaf Way II Anthology*, T. Stremlau, editor, Gallaudet University Press, 2002.

"Russian Roulette," "Solo Dining While Growing Up," and "The Promised World" in *Deaf American* Poetry, J. L. Clark, editor, Gallaudet University Press, 2009.

"If I Am at All" in *www.wordgathering.com*, Michael Nothern, editor.

"Persona Non Gratis," "Deaf Man Howls," "This Deaf-Mute Boy Who Could've," and "If I Am at All" in *www.curtdeafpoet.com*, 2010.

"Solo Dining While Growing Up," "Russian Roulette," "West Point," and "I Want to Sing" in *Deaf Lit Extravaganza*, J. L. Clark, editor, HandType Press, Minneapolis, 2013.

In spite of everything
which breathes and moves, since Doom
(with white longest hands
neatening each crease)
will smooth entirely our minds ...

—e.e. cummings

Introduction

Who am I? What am I? I am a poet.
What keeps me busy? Writing!
And what do I live on? Nothing!
In poverty I'm cheerful,
I am a prince who squanders
Arias and couplets of longing.

—"Che gelida manina" from
G. Puccini's *La Boheme*

Who am I? What am I? I am a *Deaf poet*. A Deaf poet who—in spite of everything—wishes to share the love of life and the normalities that set the differences between myself—a person who doesn't have full use of his hearing faculties—and those who do and, of course, to show the differences between myself and my deaf peers. It is an attempt to show that being deaf does not make that much of a difference on how one enjoys life. We all live by the comedy of errors. As for me, poetry does not require the faculties of my ears. It deals with my mind and soul. We all live by our absurdities, but still, we all seek happiness for our own well-being. Thus, I have every intention to illustrate what Rodolfo expresses to Mimi in the abovementioned opera:

I squander rhymes
And love songs like a lord.
When it comes to dreams and visions
And castles in the air,
I've the soul of a millionaire.

Yes, being deaf holds no bars.

Being deaf is never a bed of roses nor is it procrustean. By and large, people often think that being deaf is rather like living in the Pygmalion constraints or entrapped in the Svengali gaze making an untalented, simple girl, Trilby, the singer she never was or the Phantom of the Opera making a chorus girl, Christine, an operatic diva. So, how is it possible for a deaf person to succeed in the world of sound? And how is it possible for a deaf person to communicate with hearing people if he or she cannot hear sounds but then attempts to imitate spoken words? The culture of sound, henceforth, is totally absent. That is the essence of distrust that deaf people have toward hearing people! That is the essence of Deaf culture—espousing one's own well-being to a greater self-esteem!

> Poor Prof Higgins,
> his magic had no *boolera*,
> but my *boolera* did prevail.

> When midnight struck at the Delta Epsilon Dance,
> I was the dreamboat at my signing best!
> When midnight struck at the Tower Clock,
> I was graduated from Gallaudet at my signing best!

> *Bibbidi-bobbidi-boo!*

That is the essence of deaf people trying to impart those non-signing deaf people, to break that trance, enticing them to deny their own deafness by believing they can succeed in the hearing world.

> English has become a forbidden fruit.
> English has become a denial.
> English has become a foreign tongue

> the Deaf can't get their hands on.

And with it, poetry is not a force to reckon with. Poetry is about the moment—*carpe diem*—in life's embellishments. Poetry is often seen as a very negative medium, yet it has the most ennobling intents that are too frequency overlooked, ignored, and uneventful, because it is so magnificently minuscule for the big picture. The Deaf poetry movement is not new, however. It has been around for so long, and yet few outside the deaf community have known anything about it. Today, deaf writers and poets are widely published by deaf publishers who have anthologized them—mine included. The success of these anthologies is attested by the fact that they are widely used in many schools for the deaf and in universities that offer literature courses in deaf studies as well as disability studies.

American Sign Language as a language in and of itself is an integral communication process in the lives of Deaf people, who rely on it as their own language, their own culture, and their own livelihood. In essence, it defines and dignifies their deafness. In their own subtleties, it's their own means of survival. And so they pride themselves as being successful in their own right. There are, indeed, caustic foibles expressed that are involving and evolving in many of the poems. Some of them deal with the extreme conflicts, such as segregating themselves from non-signing deaf or hearing people.

> The smiling coach said a thing or two,
>   but there was no response—
>   Daddy's deaf too!
>
> Daddy pulled his pad and pencil
>   from his shirt pocket
>   and wrote, asking the startled coach,
>   "Please write what you just said."

This deaf-mute boy cannot play baseball.

The uniqueness of Deaf poetry as compared with centuries of poetry is twofold. First, it deals with a people that are not quite the people society is accustomed to. None can be told about deafness reflecting the differentiation in the physical makeup of the individual. Deaf people are by no means like the Elephant Man or aliens from some other unearthly places.

> What obstreperous oddity
> would disability label me—
> even with my otherwise
> able body?

Furthermore, Deaf culture is also entrenched with this sort of monomaniacal mentality—believing staunchly that all deaf people must know their own native sign language and live inside their own bubble. Henceforth, the tribalistic overtures were patronizing. Their message to the non-signers has always been that Deaf culture is the answer to greater self-esteem as a deaf individual. On the contrary, the non-signers really do not accept this notion. To them, living and working in the hearing world is a lifelong challenge, and survivability has more accountability.

> Should I be different
> or beg to differ,
> would I not
> be a part
> of this whole?

> Am I
> by nature
> so different
> by the silence
> it mutters?

And so, these poems will tell many tales, paint many pictures, and exuberate the realties of what being deaf is all about.

Second, Deaf poetry deals with the individual precepts of humanity as perceived through American Sign Language (ASL). The written word, it should be noted, is not in the form of silence, though. It is heard in subtle ways! Indeed, there is a certain silence lurking. It will all depend on how the printed words are shuffled about on each and every page. In the poem "Empty Ears," for instance, ASL is tied into the English, but then it would seem that it's a fragmented thought. In ASL, though, it is beautifully stated.

To the hearing audience of Deaf poetry, here is the gist of the matter. It is never the intent of the Deaf poetry movement to seek sympathy; rather, it sings, it dances, and it pictorializes the percepts of being human—it seeks an understanding of the bigger picture—our own senses and sensibilities. That is, it is about reaching out for such an understanding as to who we deaf people are, what we're like, how we go about, or how we deal with situations so differently than those of hearing people. Yes, there is no right or wrong. In short, Deaf poetry is about what makes Deaf people so different.

> It was a particularly uncomfortable
> moment in an elegant restaurant.
> She was surely uneasy at what she saw:
> a Deaf guy signing to his Deaf wife.

In this book, I am attempting to make several exposes to embellish, to ostracize, to epitomize, to chastise, to advocate, and to reflect with my own observations, thoughts, and visions about what it is about being deaf—and to tell my readers about it—without ever resorting to be invective but rather exonerating those realities. The negations merely expose our livelihood. I must say, I am doing this in what I believe is a very unique way of expressing them humanely. Most importantly, I am a product of my own upbringing, which is an all-encompassing experience in this comedy of errors—human errors, an ordinary life of trial-and-error—to understand the differences between myself, a deaf man in a macrocosmic hearing society and the world of sound, and my environs. It is extremely important for me to illustrate that I do have some idea what sound is, because I can hear sounds with my cochlear implant. It does not mean, though, that I can decipher what sounds I hear; nor can I determine the direction they are coming from, since I do not have that ability to distinguish them distinctively. Indeed, sound is not an integrated part of my life. Significantly, I am acculturated—a signing Deaf man who can speak understandably. Therefore, the poems were written in a homogenized process through two modes of communications strongly adhered to ASL and the spoken word as enumerated—with every effort to minimize the nuances of the grammatical structures of the English language postulated with ASL. In other words, English and ASL are written as if they interdepend. This is not to say, however, that the rules of grammar have been disregarded or ignored, but they are grammatically correct because our only means of imbibing English visually is through ASL primarily, and in most cases with speech reading—and that is, essentially visual. Historically, ASL is a product of social and educational developments, beginning in the monasteries of Spain and France in the fifteenth century. Prior to the French Revolution, the first book of sign language was compiled and published. Hence, ASL was linguistically developed and has evolved around convergences of the various grammatical structures. As attested in the poem "English," I am hopeful that my readers will appreciate the diction, the style, and the messages.

> I was up on a long hiatus—
> talking and talking,
> forgetting how easy my hands have spoken—
> still I learned to speak English.

I have included in the book poems written in English using the ASL format, such as "Coiffed Hands," to illustrate the beauty of handshapes dancing in the air in the form of a flower and how nature plays with it.

> Ah, but butterflies
> never bother
> when they
> gather from those
> mettlesome hands
> the fodder
> to nestle

Take a look at two poems: one is called "Amanuenses":

> Hail, the hands!
>   pastiche voices—
>   waggling fingers
>   clapping palms
>   hobnobbing thumbs
>   wrassling wrists
>   *et al.*

The other is "Mumpsimuses,"

> *How can I help you, sir?*

> Hey, who she?
> Me not need her help-me.
> Me, fine me.
> Help-me? For-for?

> She can't sign worth shit.

They illustrate a dichotomous calamity between two incompatible languages. They illustrate—in ASL format—a typical interaction between a signing deaf person with one who is hearing in a typical workplace trying to offer assistance but who doesn't recognize the fact that the person is deaf and continues to inquire in spoken word—which is what these two titles are in reference to. Similarly, this anthology includes poems that deal with various situations such as job discrimination, interpersonal relations, and professional people who work with the deaf. Most importantly, the poems in this book deal with the livelihoods of deaf people. In the forgoing, in piecemeal especially, the poems show how deaf people think, how they socialize, what they do, what they say, how they relate to both deaf and hearing people, and how they may be compared with other American ethnic groups in terms of cultural influences.

is for aggregating
the disenfranchised Deaf
left incommunicado
in another world—
their presence
were never
noticeable.

Finally, I also have included poems I have written about Henry Lawson (1867–1922), one of Australia's greatest poets and short story writers, whom I deeply admire. I am in total awe of the magnitude of his literary works. This deaf man was deeply imperilled by setbacks and shortcomings resulting from an upbringing beset by emotional dysfunction, extreme poverty, limited education, alcoholism, social deviance, and extreme loneliness enmeshed with distrust toward hearing people with whom he associated in business and mateships. Australia still celebrates Henry Lawson today.

This portion of the collection is dedicated to that great deaf Australian writer who dedicated his works around the lives of people who thrived in sheep towns, where shearing was a way of life, and in shantytowns, where drovers, shearers, bushmen, sundowners, roustabouts, deadbeats, and whatnot would congregate to sustain themselves collectively. His yarns and verses detail the survivability of men and women in the rawness of the Australian bush: their livelihoods, their characterizations, their mateships, and even their speech patterns! His artistry goes beyond measure—in spite of his deafness.

Each time I pick up my iPad or a book to read his verses, short stories, and biographies, or when I search the Internet for the many pictures and studies done on Henry Lawson, I am in total awe at what he did, how he did it, whom he associated with, who his mates were, and how he related to them. His legacy is beyond measure—in spite of his deafness and alcoholism.

Most remarkably, on account of his deafness, he had great difficulties getting a decent education. But it was his mother, Louisa, a pioneer in women's rights and a writer in her own right, who was instrumental in preparing him to be a writer. His greatness overwhelmed even her.

Henry Lawson was the first Australian civilian—and poet—to receive a state funeral, which was one of the largest ever attended by the public due to the immense popularity of his literary ingenuity. He was honored on the ten-dollar note (1966–1972) and on a commemorative stamp in 1949.

It seems like a worldwide rarity for one to achieve such esteem. No Deaf man or Deaf woman in the history of the world had ever received such honors as Henry Lawson. Even today in Australia, there are several annual literary and arts festivals in his honor. In addition, there are museums in Grenfell and Gulgong dedicated to him. The Henry Lawson Memorial and Literary Society, which promotes creative writing, was founded in his remembrance in 1923 in Melbourne.

Unbeknownst to many people in the literary world, Henry Lawson has set an example for all Deaf writers who have been unabashedly overlooked or shunned by those who presume wrongfully that to be a writer is an art and science—in spite of our own deafness.

I truly believe I have put together a journal of a life as a deaf man—and as a Deaf poet. The things I see, dream, think, and ponder about from what I have perceived as realities and visions to be exorcised onto the pages were presented as the highlights of happenstances—true life tales exasperatingly in search for hidden truths. In all my years, there were always cacophonic buildups waiting to flow into my fingertips, to dance on each and every page. Hopefully readers will hear the winged words that were never meant to be spoken.

Fleeing from sound
you are sound itself:
ghost of harmony,
smoke of the cry and of song.
On dark nights you come to us
to whisper the infinite
word without breath,
without lips.

—Federico Garcia Lorca, "Elegy: To Silence"

Etiology

Genesis begins
with a great big bang—
an indefinable
phantasmal nova —
Earth and heaven
    begotten!

A few whimpers
made here and there
created an innumerable
billion billion stars
    and a moon.

When the dust
fell and settled,
a man was created
in the lush,
bountiful garden—
from his rib
a woman
    begotten.

Ever so tempted
Ever so innocent
Ever the travesty—
the serpent
and the lady—
the man
has since
    sinned.

On the day
God rested
He turned my lights off
so He couldn't be heard.

Sound's Funeral

Beethoven deaf, in deafness hearing all,
Unwinds all music from sound's funeral.
                    —V. Watkins, "Discoveries"

Don't leave an epitaph—
        deaf is dead.

Unfurl me from the blackness,
        at once,
        for the depths of darkness
        is louder
        than the heights
        of silence.

Deafness
        hears all
        who creep
        into my shadow.

Amanuenses

Hark, the ears!
    the voluble mouth
    spewing microphonic
    chatterings
    cheeks
    tongue
    teeth
    throat
    lips
    et al.

Ranting rhetoric
    insipid calamity
    scowling emotions
    polemic rubric
    banal coughs
    et al.

Hail, the hands!
    pastiche voices—
    waggling fingers
    clapping palms
    hobnobbing thumbs
    wrassling wrists
    et al.

Curtis Robbins

Pratfalling fisticuffs
    winging arms
    heaving chest
    mugging faces
    jumpy eyebrows
    crab-straddling
    prancing steps
    lurking gazing eyes
    et al.

Such airborne
nebulosity
could only be
transliterated
by Deaf eyes.

Empty Ears

Consider the ear
shaped like the bass clef
but empty.

—L. Pastan, "We Come to Silence"

The musicale
of my environs
 is not
 the wrath
 of my ears
  nor
  silence
  in my eyes.

Unintentional Differential Treatment

A situation arose in the ASL classroom—
a hearing student needed assistance.
I asked if I could help;
he said no—

he'd rather wait
for my hearing assistant
to show up to help him.

Breakouts always help
when students work together—
when a problem obviously arose,
no one bothered to ask.

When teaching them to sign—
none of the students seem
to have a problem,
especially when they won't
make an effort to try
communicating with me.

Elected Silence

Elected Silence, sing to me
And beat upon my whorled ear,
Pipe me to pastures still and be
The music that I care to hear.
            —G. M. Hopkins, "The Habit of Perfection"

I care to hear
      a dancing baton:
      hyperboles of hymns
      I yearn
      to see.

I care to hear
      revolving whirls of winds
      flitting rustling leaves
      in desultory leaps,
      assailing, dancing
      embowed trees
      in silent rhapsody.

Comparison

How is this able-bodied man different from me?

What obstreperous oddity
would disability label me—
even with my otherwise
able body?

If it's my dysfunctional ears,
why compare them with those
of this hearing fellow?

Because
it's pejorative,
because other hearing fuckers think—
believe—
they're perfect.

A Question of Who

Something is amiss.
I'm left in the shadows
amid abundant conversations
at a lively party.

Some people I know
knew how to use their hands
but didn't want to be bothered.

They'd look at me
like an empty seat
with such false pretense—
        ape the enunciations,
        pout the articulations,
        macerate the pronunciations
        while whispering between
        sips and nips
        at each other's ears.

I didn't understand what they said,
of course!
I obviously didn't care to ask—
I just let it go
as if nothing happened.

If it's too much bother
to talk to me or
if I was such a bother,
why bother inviting me?

Anyway, there was nothing better to do.

Russian Roulette

Every chamber is loaded but one.

I've written letters to a lot of employers
who have advertised about
    available positions
    and if interested apply.

It was worth trying, or so I thought.

It sounded so ideal
    so perfect,
    so definitive,
    so exciting—in fact,
    too good to be true.

I waited
    and waited
    and waited
    and waited.

The ad said not to call.

Week after week
    I waited
    and waited
    and waited.

It seems
that none
of the bullet holes
on my resume
struck a chord.

Typically, my qualifying deafness
left them with a bang.

Hearing Test

Youwillsay—b a s e b a l l.

    Firefly.

Youwillsay—h o t d o g.

    Cowboy.

Youwillsay—i c e c r e a m.

    Airplane.

Locked in the airtight room,
I'm profusely sweating, and
those earphones—
a gripping vise on my head.

No end in sight.

For chrissakes,
get this motherfuckin'
thing offa me—
lemme outa here!

I can't stand it anymore!

Youwillsay—r a i l r o a d.

The Mangal

Rooting tendrils of tenacious mangroves
reaching deep in the putrid muck,
holding and feeding
out of decay-rich, briny,
inhospitable swamp beds.

The mangal—
a mangrove brush
impenetrably entangled
impenetrably entwined
impenetrably enmeshed
reaching deep in the putrid muck
holding and feeding
out of the decay-rich briny
inhospitable swamp beds.

*I was wading through
the tidewater trying
most vainly to get out—
it's always that fear
that a scheming crocodile,
hiding under the roots
of arachnoid snares,
swaggers its way
to snatch me.*

Laborious mangroves—
their tenacity clustering
brush brethren,
hordes of stipules
sticking together
against the whirling swells—
the raging of the unpredictable sea.

The woven-webbed mangroves—
no refuge from dangers
from creeping neap tides
or murky jungle
swamps that leave
little for safety—
the mangrove crabs
mercilessly savor
the putrid muck.

The woven-webbed mangroves—
it's always that fear
between those roots
like the clasping
manacles readily
snagging and cuffing
my feet.
The mangrove crabs
mercilessly savor
the putrid muck.

An allured crocodile could be lurking
beneath the ravishing sweeps
of dancing mangroves
rampaging the hidden sun
over the height—
awaiting for me.

The mangal—
even in its loveliness—
its intimacy is beyond reach.

West Point

Suddenly, in full volume,
my hearing aid picked up
a Sousa marching tune—
it was that loud too.

Suddenly, on B&W television,
a line of men—
white sashes crossed
their gray chests
with centered buckles;
white trousers kicked
  left, right,
  left, right,
  left, right;
high hats with dark prickly plumes
pranced on top
with shouldered, bayoneted rifles—
marched smartly
across the screen.

The vividness of
the Dress Parade
at West Point
has entered nearly
every dream
I've dreamed
since.

One day,
Dad asked me,
"What do you want be when you grow up?"

I stood smartly,
saluted him,
and replied,
"Go t'West Point,
Daddy."

He chuckled (to mask misgivings
about my deafness)
and replied,
"No, Curt,
you can't hear.
Don't you understand that?"

No.

Persona Non Gratis

I'm here
at your service
in your employ,
though possibly overqualified
as compared with most others
in the same position before.

I'm here
at your service,
hired to do what only so few can do—
they've moved on,
passing through
the storied walls.

I'm here
at your service
to perform routines
like recipes
efficiently functional
to keep satiation smiling
at intolerable situations—
just simply doing all it takes
to make myself look good.

I'm here
at your service.
The plot only thickens.
When things are done,
ingratitudes pay.

I just was never appreciated.

Solo Dining While Growing Up

My whole family sat down at the dinner table

There was always
    a lot to eat from corner to corner.

There was always conversation
    between forks and spoons.

There was always conversation
    between glasses and cups.

There was always conversation
    between napkins.

There were always
    empty plates and empty bowls.

But the knife that lay between them all—
    from mouth to ear,
    from mouth to eye—

        cut me off.

I Want to Sing

I want to sing the blues
in words that no music
    could tune.

I want to sing jazz
in words that no music
    could tune.

They're soulful but
not like those from the streets of New Orleans,
from the cotton fields
around the Delta.

The heat is on me,
snapping my fingers.

No cane flute to whistle
but hurricane winds;
rains dillydally,
drip-dropping on my head,
rummaging for rhythm,
moaning jazz,
mumbling blues.

Midnight! Moonlight!

A thousand stars twinkle-tinkle.
I want to sing the blues
in words that no music
    could tune.

I want to sing jazz
in words that no music
     could tune.

Midnight! Moonlight!

They're soulful, but
my ears could never be set to the tunes.

The heat is on me.
No piano to tap but
the make-believe
twang plucks.

No cane flute to whistle
but hurricane winds;
rains dillydally,
drip-dropping on my head,
mustering for muted meanings,
moaning jazz,
mumbling blues.

Midnight! Moonlight!

No Rhythm, They Say

Some people say
        because I'm deaf
        I've no rhythm.

I might confess to that,
        but then I shan't
        out of the misnomer in the logic
        about rhythm.

Why, don't you know
        that everything we do
        in life is done in the rhythm?

Does it matter whether you hear it or not?

Now, of course, it's not by
        the beat of the drum—
        not every be-bobing dum-dee-dum
        is in the rhythm—

        it takes a sound mind
        to imbibe and imbue
        with rhythm.

Once I get the knack
        of doing something right,
        the logic of the action
        concludes the intent
        of the rhythm.

That's logically sound, yes?

And so, it takes rhythm—
>there's nothing
>my mind wouldn't hear
>that rings

>the twangs of Silence's rhythm.

The Metronome

I blew the cornet
    but was easily out of breath.
I skedaddled the clarinet,
    but my lips befuddled the beak.
I plucked a banjo
    but couldn't drum up a tune.
I sat in the orchestra
    but couldn't decipher the clef.
I tried out for the choir,
    but my voice sounded
    like a mewing gull
    choking on a squid.
I strummed a guitar,
    but Dad hollered,
    "That's enough!"

But then Uncle gave me
    that metronome
    sitting on the shelf.

I couldn't help be curious,

watching the pendulum sway
    back and forth
    back and forth
    back and forth

like a thin deboned *Handshape One* sway-saying,
    "No way
    no way
    no way."

Look down
and see the beggars at your feet
Look down
and show some mercy if you can
Look down
and see the sweepings of the street
Look down, look down,
upon your fellow man!

—"Look Down" from *Les Miserables* by Herbert Kretzmer

Guttersnipe

Prof Higgins found Eliza
at her Cockney best
selling flowers
for her keeps
at the Covent Garden.

Prof Higgins found a specimen
in her rawest moment,
utterly unprepared
to be his beguiled Cinderella
without that
bibbidi-bobbidi-boo—
she's what he dreams
to make her think
it's a *bibbidi-bobbidi-boo*!

With all that *boolera*,
his professorial cockiness
never really brought about the magic.

When midnight struck at the Ascot races,
Eliza was at her Cockney best!
When midnight struck at the Embassy Ball,
Eliza was at her Cockney best!

Bibbidi-bobbidi-boo!

All that *boolera*
made her unhappy ever after.

Curtis Robbins

I was born in the gutters of NYC,
raised in the woods of LI—
living in the confines of comfort—
warm home,
plentiful food,
nightly baths,
clean clothes,
denigrating public schools.

Prof Higgins found a specimen
in my rawest moments
in those lifelong never-ending
speech therapy sessions
with all my inborn
mouthful of marbles.

Poor Prof Higgins,
his magic had no *boolera*,
but my *boolera* did prevail.

When midnight struck at the Delta Epsilon Dance,
I was the dreamboat at my signing best!
When midnight struck at the Tower Clock,
I was graduated from Gallaudet at my signing best!

Bibbidi-bobbidi-boo!

They Call Me by the Labels

I

Hearing people have
an uncanny ability,
a tendency
to put labels on everybody—
anybody they
hardly know.

It doesn't matter
who they are
or what they do
or where they are;
they have the propensity
to profess
their idiosyncratic ability
to indisputably
put labels
on those
unlike themselves.

What do you think I am?

I'll bet
you've a preconceived notion
of what you think I am
already;
it's most definitely
a negation
from what
I am really.

How—
if anything—
would it make a difference
to convince you
otherwise?

To think
I owe an
explanation
to make the difference
knowing nothing
would change
your mind.

So, why
should I
make the difference?

Call me what you will.

Whatever label you give me,
chances are
you'd be wrong;
the misconception will
most definitely
misrepresent the inevitable—

I am what I am.

II

My Deaf friends,
undoubtedly,
even they have labels

for those in the same circles
and those out in different circles.

Some they know,
and a few they don't.

It never matters
even in the small world
they meander in.

It doesn't matter
who they are—
the propensity
to profess
their idiosyncratic ability
to put insipid labels
even on their
own Deaf friends.

Some who don't sign as well,
some who never did,
and some who tried so hard
but never mastered
the language of the hands.

God forbid
they should talk!

Anathema!

The labels
such Deaf friends use!

To Deaf

Deaf—
>Am I such
>an inquisitive misanthrope
>whose voice is louder and rowdier
>than sounds arousing
>curiosity?

Deaf—
>I once sat by
>the orchestra pit
>in a theater
>watching dancing feet
>gracefully tip the stage
>while her liquescent arms
>softly stroked the air
>like flaunting branches
>from swinging trees
>in whispering winds
>at the height of
>the blithe
>violin bows.

Deaf—
>When asleep
>I awaken in dreams
>hearing capricious poetics
>from the flow of hands
>dancing
>in the cadence
>of deviant voices.

Deaf—
> Can words
> persevere
> without the genteel hands
> even with enraged voices?

Deaf—
> Am I such an ostentatious
> meditative misanthrope
> whose words dance on the page
> at the heights
> of deprecating hands
> in the verses
> of impassioned
> voices?

Impudent Woman

Impudent woman—
I never intended
to take it out on her
and tell it like it is.

Her disruptive pomposity—
she toyed me coquettishly
dancing to her folly
and laughing quite jollily—

only for a time
the floor was hers
until my Deaf wife
came by.

Impudent woman—
a wicked hearing married
woman—
stunned by her own subterfuge,
saddened.

Tearfully listless
with no smiles to throw
withered among friends—
realizing I quite simply
adore my Deaf wife.

(C-L-U-B)

is for aggregating
the disenfranchised Deaf
left incommunicado
in another world—
their presence
never
noticeable.

is in town at night
on an abandoned street
with a parking lot
quickly filling up,
overshadowed
by vivid, spidery hands
rushing to roost.

is a long, dark flight upstairs—
lit by a filth-heated,
dust-coated, ancient,
incandescent light
hanging indistinctly
above the door—
     its luminance
     is barely
     noticeable.

The dark,
mildewed,
dead air precipitated
the stairway, leads
the deafening, silent crowds
through the open
dead-bolted door.

is away from the real home
with all that makes up
     a real home:
     a playroom,
     a kitchen,
     a dining room,
     a living room—
          a huge family room
          that has never been
          exceptionally
          especially
          noticeable.

is smoky,
stale-beer,
rancid,
crowded with
livid, grappling hands
shoulder-to-shoulder,
>   sweaty,
>   mangy
from the idle excitation
of endless sign-talking
under the blast-bright
fluorescent lights
with a single ceiling fan
lazing a whiff—
>   its breeze
>   is barely
>   noticeable.

is away from the real home.
The whole family is all on the floor
catching hand-flies,
>   fluttering
>   with people-bumping,
>   spilling,
>   beer splats,
>   wine-dips,
>   and cola-smacks.

Curtis Robbins

Hearing children
hang out
by the coat closet
hiding from
the damning,
knuckle-snapping,
finger-slapping,
cackle-ribbing,
guttural-throaty voices—
kibitzing and giggling,
attempting to take the gaggle
out of the painful humdrum
of their disjointedness—
    Deaf parents
    are persistently,
    painstakingly
    watchful.

Deaf children
rollick together,
running about
in between
the clamored floor,
making mockery
of themselves,
commingling
for innocent troubles
to kill boredom.

Their impishness
is hardly
noticeable.

is the Deaf gathering,
an escapade from daily realities
laughing at their own
indignant pratfalls,
forgetting pain,
extrapolating ire,
nipping and biting
at each other's backs;
everyone took notice.

Ain't No Law

There are laws that make us
    legally deaf—
        and still, no knows
        what to do with us.

There are laws that make us
    schools so we can see
    what teachers say,
        and still, we're underachieved.

There are laws that make us
    closed captions to decode
    what they're saying on television
    and the movies,
        and still, we missed the gist.

There are laws that make us
    jobs so we can work
    just like those hearing guys,
        and still, we're underemployed.

There are laws that make us
    telephones, cell phones, and videophones
    so we can communicate
    just like those hearing guys,
        and still, we're ubiquitously disconnected.

There are laws that make us
    colleges so we can
    maybe, just maybe
    be professionals
    just like those hearing guys—
        and still, we're underrated.

There are laws that make us—
    there are laws that made them make.

Shit, man.

There are laws for everything—
    we still fight every fucking time
    for our rights to every fucking thing.

So, how come there ain't no law about being Deaf?

Dummy

I ain't no dummy, and dare you call me one,
I'm no different than anyone else
So why the rancor?

You ignoramus,
I didn't get this far acting like one,
nor was I straitjacketed for being different.

Where did you get such a cockamamie thought,
that mind and sound are cranially symbiotic?

I'm never at a loss—
you're just acting as if anything you say
I wouldn't understand
and what I say
would be hard for anyone
to understand.

Come on, man.
Stop the nonsense.
I'm just another cog like you,
so don't try winding me down
        because I'm deaf
        or just because
        you're hearing.

The Staged Harlot

In this newly rehabbed theater,
a barstool, front center stage,
spotlight on the dusty ambience.

She sheepishly swaggers
all her weight
toward the stool
in her regular street clothes—
hardly distinguishable from
those of an ordinary lady.

She hand-wiped the dust off the stool,
rubbed her fingers with a smirk,
climbed on;
her miniskirt rode back
and then crossed her bare legs.

The light shone on the shins
of her crossed naked legs,
pandering her off-colored, high-heeled,
cork platform slippers.

She was there to tell stories about her johns,
discussing the art of her sexuality
and, if anything, her
johnny-come-lately episodes.

Her painted face couldn't hide the wrinkles.
Her lips red and dark,
as if the spotlight missed a spot,
were hardly moving.
Her nervousness couldn't hide her peerless presence.

Curtis Robbins

She searched for a smoke,
but her john couldn't
(or wouldn't) appear.

I was too far back in the front center row.
I couldn't fathom what she said.
The beacon from her shins—
her pandering, crossed, naked legs—
sent a distracting,
convoluted message.

Gawk

Have you ever seen the ugly sight
of people gawking, especially at you?

It's downright ridiculous, but
I was amused,
so I gawked back at the gawker!

It was a particularly uncomfortable
moment in an elegant restaurant.
She was surely uneasy at what she saw:
a Deaf guy signing to his Deaf wife.

I had to reciprocate
as if I'd never seen anyone behave
like that before—
an utter disgrace on my part.

This pompous, elegant elderly lady …
she was something else,
but you know what?

I wonder
if she had the same
thoughts about me.

On Alchemizing Deafness

Psst. Psst. Presto! *Psst.*
Let me tell you a tale of wits;
you'd laugh and laugh
until you tear—
you'd never dare ask
and laugh again!

I'm not on a wizard's quest
to change
amethyst to gold.

Psst. Psst. Presto! *Psst.*
Let me tell you the truth;
you'd grunt and groan
until you tear—
you'd never dare ask
and grunt again.

I'm not even on a wizard's quest
to change stone deafness
to a golden ear.

Psst. Psst. Presto! *Psst.*
Let me tell you a tale of lies;
you'd laugh and laugh
until you tear—
you'd never dare ask
and laugh again.

> *Shush! Shush!* Say no word!
> *Slap! Slap!* Show no hands!

Money flows
out of desperate pockets.

Desolate voices shout
out of desperate souls.

Signing hands fly
out of desperate hearts.

Still, money flows
out of desperate pockets.

> *Shush! Shush!* Say no word!
> *Slap! Slap!* Show no hands!

Psst. Psst. Presto! *Psst.*
Let me tell you what I am;
you'd step aside,
far away until you tear—
you'd never dare
slap my hands again.

> *Shush! Shush!* Say no word!
> *Slap! Slap!* Show no hands!

My child is deaf;
what do I do?
Here's my money;
do what you have to do—
make my child hearing.

Weep and weep
until you tear!

Psst. Psst. Presto! *Psst.*
Let me tell you the truth;
you'd grunt and groan
until you tear—
you'd never dare ask
and grunt again.

Curtis Robbins

I am Deaf—
I am fine!

What would your money do then?

Weep and weep
until you tear.

Weep and weep—
you can't just slap my hands!

What your money buys
they will make.

What they make
may never work.

What you vainly want
may never happen.

Psst. Psst. Presto! *Psst.*
Let me tell you a tale of lies;
you'd weep and weep
until you tear—
you'd never dare ask
and weep again.

    Shush! Shush! Say no word!
    Slap! Slap! Show no hands!

Psst. Psst. Presto! *Psst!*
Let me tell you again
what I am;
you'd step aside,
far away—
you'd never dare slap
my hands again.

Weep and weep
until you tear

You've just paid the price
with your child's deafness—
so have I
all life long.

    Shush! Shush! Say no word!
    Slap! Slap! Show no hands!

Psst. Psst. Presto! *Psst.*
Let me tell you the truth;
you'd grunt and groan
until you tear—
you'd never dare ask
and weep again.

Nothing will make
a golden ear
out of stone
deafness.

The Promised World

I nearly was born
without hearing a sound
and was promised the world
with things to come
if I had adapted—
imitating sound.

I was tutored with sound
and was promised the world
if I learned to deal
with the hearing aid—
thinking and believing
I'm hearing everything—
only to ask where and
what they were.

I was raised
and was promised the world
if I behaved
as if I didn't know
the difference—
only to wonder why.

I was educated at Gallaudet
and was promised the world
if I learned ASL
and believed in the future
scintillating on a silver platter—
if only I heard beforehand.

I was raised
to think and reason like a man—
and was promised the world
that I'd be a better man—
if only they knew.

Scrawling

I've been scrawling in the labyrinth of words
forgetting time
seeking shelter,
hunting for food,
groping for thought,
trying to survive the loss.

    What my eyes and my ears couldn't perceive,
    stagnation persevered,
    the imminent urging
    an adage left in the glade,
    an entailment left for sniffing,
    a cadaver in an empty manger.

I've been scrambling on a mountain of words
forgetting time,
seeking a sublet,
hunting for a gaunt spoon,
groping for thought,
trying to survive the imperceptibles.

    What my eyes and my ears couldn't perceive,
    stagnation persevered,
    the imminent urging
    an adage left on the street,
    empty papers left for grabbing,
    a cadaver in a wired basket.

I've been scribbling in the shadow of words
forgetting time,
seeking light,
hunting for an image,
groping for thought,
trying to survive the unimaginable.

What my eyes and my ears couldn't perceive,
stagnation persevered,
the imminent urging
an adage left in my mind,
caprices left for forking,
a cadaver on an empty plate.

English

I wasn't up from a residential school
cut off from the real world
way out in the boondocks
far from hearing people,
far from tall buildings,
far from home,

locked behind the invisible wall
with only green grass,
    loitering squirrels,
    pecking birds,
    tall crowding trees,
    familiar buildings,
    and everybody danced
    with their hands.

Only there
the gods
that spoke,
only the Gods
that signed—
they knew English,

and the little angels
were merely in flight.

I wasn't up
in an isolated institution,
nor was I spirited
just like another little angel
merely in flight
out in the open sky.

Curtis Robbins

I was up from PS 40
on Staten Island
in the middle of town,
too busy signing
and mimicking.
Teacher spoke English but didn't sign.
Principal spoke English but didn't sign.
The class just babbled airlessly and handedly.

I was up on a long hiatus—
talking and talking,
forgetting how easy my hands have spoken—
still I learned to speak English.

Mom spoke English.
Dad spoke English.
My sibs too.
Grandma and Grandpa too.
My aunts and uncles too.
And so did my cousins.

My neighbors did.
My buddies did.
Even the guys
who bullied me did.

I've been reprimanded in English.
I've been scatted in English.
I've been punished in English.

I've ridden the subways,
taken the public buses,
rode taxicabs
watching tall buildings
point up so high,
sweeping clouds by.

I've walked Park Avenue.
I've skipped on Broadway.
I've rolled around at Central Park.
I've raced up and down
Fifth Avenue,
bumping into people
who were bumped
countless times.

I was carted around in Grand Union.
I've escalated up and down in Macy's.
I've crawled under the hangered clothes in Gimbel's.
I've gotten lost in Orbach's, hiding inside clothes drawers.
I've fogged the windows of
Bloomingdale's at Christmastime.

Still I've gotten so many lickings
for being a good kid
doing the wrong things—
Mommy hollered at me
    in English.

I spoke English.
I lip-read English.
I read English.
I wrote in English.

I've been upped from the public schools
    where hearing kids laughed and shouted,
    where teachers had pointers and chalk,
        exerting authority,
    and all I knew was English

until I learned,
and still love, ASL—
it never silenced my tongue.

I've been upped from Gallaudet
>   when ASL and English were a pair.
I've taught at Gallaudet
>   when ASL and English splintered.
I've taught ASL everywhere,
>   yet the hearing demanded signed English.

English has become a forbidden fruit.
English has become a denial.
English has become a foreign tongue

the Deaf can't get their hands on.

The Silver Fox in Front of the House

Once in a while
at the nick of dawn,
just when ready
to enter a working day,
I would greet
a passing silver fox.

"Why, good morning, dear.
Hope the cubs
are doing dandy!"

The silver fox
quickly stiffened with
a cautious cold stare—

a quick sniff
just as quick,
drifted by
was her usual,
tersely demurred
morning greeting.

Well,
one morning
there was
a squashed silver fox
in the middle of the road
in front of the house
as I fetched
the morning papers.

Curtis Robbins

Slow nocturnes,
quick flashed lights
that sped by
did make her
sly no more.

Newspapers
hardly ever mention
such tragedy
naturally.

... hear me for my cause, and be silent, that you may hear: believe me for mine honor, and have respect to mine honor, that you may believe: censure me in your wisdom, and awake your senses, that you may the better judge.

— William Shakespeare, *Julius Caesar* (act 3, scene 2)

Shticks

A first-grade teacher really didn't want me in her classroom.
She'd make a scapegoat out of me for everything
that went wrong in the classroom. She even had
feces rolled in wax paper—looking like a Tootsie Roll—
accusing me for putting it in a lunch box on the school bus.

Some kid really didn't want me as a playmate.
He, like the other bunch of guys, simply wouldn't let me play.
Once they played stickball in the schoolyard;
a kid hit a high pop fly—a pink Spalding ball I caught with one hand.
The other kid kicked me for being a better fielder.

A classmate in junior high really didn't like me.
He was always a mischievous class jester.
Everything he said or did always cracked everybody up.
Even the teacher couldn't help laughing at his shtick—
even when he snipped my hearing aid cord from behind.

Two rabbis couldn't teach me anything.
The Hebrew language was so easy to learn,
but chanting "Shalom Alechim" was quite difficult.
I once aspired to become a rabbi because
There were so many Jewish Deaf who needed one.
No one believed me.

A high school coach really didn't want me in his classroom,
nor allowed me to join any team sport he coached or taught.
During a Greco-Roman wrestling class
He matched me with a guy much taller and heavier.
I pinned him with a half nelson—still, I flunked.

Even the girls in high school wouldn't let me date them.
Why be a butt of a joke? they figured.
I asked one to go with me to the senior prom.
She declined with a smirk and rolled her eyes—
she never went, I heard. Neither did I.

Some students at college didn't want to talk to me
because I didn't know sign language then.
They made fun of me as if I wouldn't understand.
They mocked me—calling me a *garrulous hippopotamus*—
yet I thrived as a sign language teacher.

And even *the whole world is wide*.
I'm so sure I'm not alone—in every culture
there are shticks that impugn
even the slightest deviants
who tried so hard to be normal.

Daydreams

In my early school days
I learned to be a daydreamer—
often participating in class
was such a waste of time!

Alice and Jerry readers
were rather easy to read,
but Teacher kept telling me
to follow along—
I hadn't the slightest notion
where in the book to look!
I just kept reading it
over and over to myself,
and then I glimpsed at
the penmanship cards
above the blackboard.

Teacher called upon me
to read the next line!

Huh? What?
Where? Huh?

I was still on page 3,
the class on page 10.

"Curtis! You're not paying attention!"

How was I supposed
to know if I couldn't hear
anyone reading aloud?

Even then, in junior high
I became a pretty good daydreamer.
I began seeing abstract imageries
looking at the scheme of things
around the classroom
and out the window—
still, participating in class
was such a waste of time!

The class was reading
The Devil and Daniel Webster
from a literature book,
but Teacher kept telling me
to follow along—
I had the slightest notion
where in the book to look!
I read the story
in its entirety and
watched the clouds
meander across
the morning sky.

Teacher called upon me
to read the next paragraph
about Webster's encounter
with this peculiar stranger!

Huh?   What?
Where? Huh?

I was still on page 213,
the class on page 216.

"Curtis! You're not paying attention!"

What was I supposed to do?
Teacher knew I couldn't hear.
Even Principal originally presumed
I was a retard—
not that I couldn't learn.
They didn't want to be
bothered with my handicaps.

Yet in high school
I was already an excellent daydreamer—
any thought that came to mind
was worth implosive sensualities
in my wildest dreams.
Well, participating in class
was such a waste of time!

The class delved into *Julius Caesar.*
Teacher, in his song-and-dance routine,
recited Mark Antony's speech in attempts
to introduce Shakespeare.

The class followed along;
I was totally lost,
but Teacher kept telling me
to follow along—
I hadn't the slightest notion
where in the book to look!
I read the play
one act at a time, and
in between watching
how Teacher
zigzagged around the room.

Teacher called upon me
to read what Brutus did
before his suicide.

Curtis Robbins

Huh? What?
Where? Huh?

I was still on page 112,
the class on page 128.

"Curtis! You're not paying attention!"

Et tu, Brute?

Deaf Peddlers

... They sell the hollow
of their hands.
> —Rainier Maria Rilke, "The Beggars"

All day long (sometimes at night, too)
on the streets
or under
the subways
or at the getaways,
airports,
bus depots,
train stations,
or at the eateries—
they weren't even hungry.

They just went around
handing out manual alphabet cards

    I AM DEAF
    PLEASE HELP

then return to collect them again
expecting some change with it.

After a good day's round,
they count
their blessings.

When they get back to the Deaf club,
they rant and rant and rant,
sick and tired of hearing people
feeling sorry for Deaf people.

Damned

Why should I right his wrong?
When I have come so far
and struggled for so long.
If I speak, I am condemned.
If I stay silent, I am damned!
    —"Who Am I?" (*Les Miserables)*

Born to be free
even without
freedom to hear
embattling words
bombarding walls,
condemning
those who speak—

even without
freedom to hear
encouragement
to sign is walled.

If I am not heard
and cannot be seen,
then I am damned!

He's Deaf, for Chrissakes!

The lightbulb glows
    when the sky darkens.

The jack-o-lantern laughs
    when the candle dims.

The gourd keeps shape
    when gracefully empty.

The balloon dances airily
    when untethered to ascend.

The cicada shells cling
    when the seventeenth year embarks.

The mind beacons
    when latent ears listen
    and rambunctious eyes seek.

Deaf man stridulates
    when ignorance peaks.

Deaf man cries out
    when impertinence meets.

Deaf man sees
    when malice impugns.

He's deaf, for chrissakes!

This Deaf-Mute Boy Who Could've

S. F. W.

There was once
    a five-and-a-half-year-old precocious Deaf kid
    who was taken to try out
    for a Little League baseball team.

He was among the fifty-plus kids
    whose daddies thought their sons were the best.

The Deaf kid tried out for catcher
    and turned out to be the best—
    even his daddy thought so too.

The coaches were quite impressed
    by the Deaf kid's abilities
    to bat, catch, and throw.

The coaches gathered
    to declare the choicest of the bunch.

Names of each kid were called,
    but the Deaf kid—
    who was so good
    was, for sure, the catcher
    for the new team—
    stood waiting,
    knowing he was really so good.

A few times the Deaf kid's name
    was called,
      but each time
      there was no response.

A coach finally came over,
    asked the Deaf kid,
    "Where's your daddy?"
    The Deaf kid waved for Daddy to come.

The smiling coach said a thing or two,
    but there was no response—
    Daddy's deaf too!

Daddy pulled his pad and pencil
    from his shirt pocket
    and wrote, asking the startled coach,
    "Please write what you just said."

This deaf-mute boy cannot play baseball.

No Fairy Tales

No fairy tales—
no fairy tales at all.
None to remember.
None to retell.

But I was amused
when I read them
as a kid.

And yes, I watched them
on television too.

My father was no king
        nor my mother a queen.
My brother was no prince
        nor my sisters princesses.
        Nor were there witches—
        only lonely old ladies
        wandering about the gutters.
        Nor were there beggars—
        only drunkards
        panning for another shot.

There were no black cauldrons
or monstrous dragons around.

No. No fairy tales—
no fairy tales at all.
None to remember.
None to retell.

I'd tell you of New York City subways—
    hardly tunnels of fear.
I'd tell you of great bridges over rivers—
    too strong for scary thresholds.
I'd tell you of magnificent skyscrapers—
    high and glassy for romantic castles.
I'd tell you of fantastic rides and
    adventuresome drives
        in cars
        and trucks
        and buses
        and trains
        and planes—
more nice and comfortable
than a sleigh, a buggy, or a saddle.

If I had to decide which fairy tale
    would be conceivably,
        reasonably,
        unalterably
    a life with my loving wife
        with bushy brown hair
        and two great kids—
        wild and woolly—
        eager to run.

No. No fairy tales—
no fairy tales at all.
None to remember.
None to retell.

Who would believe
hereafter that
we'd live ever so happily?

Deaf Man Howls

Long, loud, and cantankerous is the howl
raised by the deaf-mute! It has to be if
he wishes to be heard and listened to.
—Albert Ballin, *The Deaf-Mute Howls*

The universality of ASL
was never the remedy—
diversity among us
made divisions
in our own crumbled Babel.

We've estranged ourselves
from the cantankerous world
and muted our own silence.

Still we howl.

The remedy was never
the ultimate solution;
laws were made
like rules in the institute
to make us
deviously divisive
and indecisive.

We've sought out
for escapades
to avoid taxing volitions
for the better.

Still we howl.

The solution has always
been within us,
but its invincibility
left us mucking
in perpetuating battles.

We've gagged and screamed
at each other
for righteous claim
to glory, but no one
staked the claim to divinity.

Still we howl.

Tonight as in every bitter sunset
with the hazy full moon
there still will be more,
Deaf Man howls.

We've done it so many times
before, and still there won't be
anyone there for the chase.

Still we howl.

If I Am at All

… obtaining nirvana is like locating silence
— *The Dharma Bums* by Jack Kerouac

There have been times
of questioning
the state of my being.

The impropriety
of my individuation
in the hearing society—
conform or else?

Should I be different
or beg to differ,
would I not
be a part
of this whole?

Am I
by nature
so different
by the silence
it mutters?

Is deafness
like death,
so remote
yet so imminent?

At the Slightest Sleight of Hand

In just a moment,
when suddenly
things change—
it was so sudden,
beyond description,
beyond imagination,
I am still wondering
just how it ever came about

at the slightest sleight of hand.

Scratching my head
every so often,
trying to fit,
puzzle pieces—
the thoughts that rattle
persistently,
the thoughts that agitate
consistently

at the slightest sleight of hand.

Until a potpourri of old memories
start to fall in place
just when things are so incomparable,
just when things are so remarkable—
I simply can't fathom
just how a pebble
fallen from the sky
hit my head

at the slightest sleight of hand.

All at the moment
when I never expected it,
things have begun to change.
It wasn't even displacement;
it wasn't even misplacement
of just a misbegotten thought
or even a misbegotten fantasy.
It was all spur of the moment

at the slightest sleight of hand.

It's so wickedly ticklish
that this had just happened.
I simply can't even imagine
what I'm supposed to do next.
I'm uttering spitting stammers.
I'm sputtering at a loss
for sensibilities
that are so wickedly ticklish

at the slightest sleight of hand.

Ain't Nobody There?

No, there ain't nobody around.

I could be standing next to a guy
who's hearing a PA announcement.
I could tell if someone is making
an announcement but not what he's saying.
If I ask this guy what was said,
he'd say—as always—
"Nothing important"
or
"Not sure what he's saying"
or
"I dunno."

No, there ain't nobody around.

I could be standing next to a lady
who's hearing a commotion.
I could tell if something is happening
and everyone is running and screaming.
If I ask this lady what is going on,
she'd say—as always—
"Something has happened"
or
"Oh, something or other"
or
"I don't know."

No, there ain't nobody around.

I'm all alone in the middle
of a thrashing, bashing crowd
on the run like a parade in disarray.

Curtis Robbins

There's no knowing
where to go
or
what to find
or
who to ask.

No, there's ain't nobody around.

I'm all alone in the band.
There ain't nothing to toot or woof a horn for,
and
there ain't nothing to pluck or strum a guitar,
and
there ain't nothing to bow or rappel a bass,
and
there ain't nothing to dance or clap about,
and
no way could I sing.

No, there ain't nobody around.

Sounds around always abound
so noisily so. I cannot know
what they are
or
where they come from
or
wonder why people are
always running about
and can't tell me
what they're all about.

No, there ain't nobody around.

Mumpsimuses

Hello, sir.
How can I help you?

No, me ask-you? No.
Me look lost?
Me look frightened?
Me look stupid?
Me not!

No, no thank-you.
Me, fine me.
Help-me? For-for?

How can I help you, sir?

Hey, she tell-me what?
Me don't-understand me.
Doesn't-matter.
She not understand me.

Hello, sir.
How can I help you, sir?

No, me ask-you? Why?
Me look lost?
Me look frightened?
Me look stupid?
Me not.

No, no thank-you.
Me, fine me.
Why-not write back-and-forth she?
She stupid, she.

Curtis Robbins

How can I help you, sir?

Hey, who she?
Me not need her help-me.
Me, fine me.
Help-me? For-for?

She can't sign worth shit.

Grassroots

Hidden in jungles of bricks, slabs, and poured concrete,
shuffling, scuffing, and buffing about the walks and streets,
rushing, pushing, and shoving in misdirected traffic,
running the day,
dropping by on conveyer belts,
burning rubber on bumper rides,
scuffling between carpeted calls,
waiting on line for tattered,
unemployment checks.

Bare essentials abundant,
hardly satisfying meals,
unnourishing nourishment
harbored on subway crates,
housing under compartmental corrugations,
resting for another day,
pushing mountainous bundles
on swindled, forgotten shopping carts,
searching for usable essentials.

Homeless, shameless, unemployed hands
already trained, job-ready, and highly recommended,
utterly disenfranchised, disqualified qualifiables,
scrambling to scrape the bottomed essences,
quick to pan out for flipped out pennies and dimes
for delectable bites from greasy spoons,
sipping evaporated coffee from inked cups,
shoveling parched rice from cracked containers,
sporking for decent satiation in the dark, cold alley.

School days are a-wastin'.
Teachers don't know what life is about.
Brainy guys and dressy cats ain't nothin' but spoiled brats.

Books won't make my hands dirty.
Takin' big tests don't mean a damned thin'.
If I get into trouble, who's gonna care?
Momma or Pop ain't gonna get me.
Still I'm stuck in school.
Ain't got no place else to go.

Dingy apartments crowding hoards of wearable rags
barely fitting hungry children crying fitfully.
Momma ain't around to pamper.
Dirty dishes piling up in the sink,
mildewed fridge melting ice,
frying pans cooking saucepans on the cold stove,
stewpot sitting half-full for splattered spoons
waiting for scoops for empty mouthfuls,
hungering for bellies full of laughter.

O for the dreadful life of the grassroots!
O lowly grassroots Deaf
on the lowest rung of the totem pole,
posted on shards of words from home,
running against impartial time
for ungainly chances,
for wasted essentials
with tattered paychecks
while vaulted in obscurity.

Music

I grew up
a hearing aid user,
wearing it like
eyeglasses,
mascara,
and red nose,
white, red lips
rainbow wig,
loud baggy jumpsuit,
and oversized shoes—
except no one had the nerve to laugh at me!

I could never describe
sounds—
I just hear them.
No point asking me
what they were,
what made them,
and from which direction—
I'd only ask you that,
not out of curiosity
because it's something
I heard and
I really want to know.

Everywhere I go
I see people jiving
when they listen to music—
lip-synching,
carousing hips,
tapping feet,
snapping fingers,
gyrating heads—

sensational nonchalance
in precipitous moments
with such things that look like
bilateral hearing aids plugged in!!

Hmm, I wonder.

Now I have
a cochlear implant—
sounds are definitely quite different
from a hearing aid.

I still can't fully describe
sounds—
I just hear them.
No point asking me
what they were,
what made them,
and from which direction—
I'll still ask you that,
not out of curiosity
because it's something
I heard and
I really want to know—
or I might know
those sounds
without even
realizing it.

Every time I hear something musical,
I do things
I've never done before,
only with childlike awe—
listening to the musicality
of such music,
lip-synching,
carousing my hips,
tapping my feet,

snapping my fingers,
gyrating my head.
Even my own grown, hearing kids were laughing at me!

Hmm, I wonder!

They never ever saw me like this before.

If asked what I've just heard,
I'd equivocally tell you
I still could never describe the music at all.

Coiffed Hands

My dissipated hands have
been supplanted in the air
like weed seeds deposited
from avian droppings,
wind-blown yet succinctly fallen
stepped on, then scrapped off
or squashed, then trickled off
elsewhere—
somewhere.

Anywhere?

Drone bees,
honey bees,
and bumblebees
extract nectars
gathered from
splaying hands—
disposed,
deposited,
delivered,
to the vaults
of reconnaissance.

Ah, but butterflies
never bother
when they
gather from those
mettlesome hands
the fodder
to nestle

while ladybugs
gather from those
reconnoitering hands
the gossips
for the cuspidor,

awaiting morphed words
for exhilarating hands
combed and winged,
imbibed from vaulted
regiments
of emblazoned
whirlwinds
in a perfumed
garden.

I was painfully shy, extremely sensitive, about my deafness, about my lack of education, my surroundings, my clothes, slimness, and paleness, my 'h's', handwriting, grammar, pronunciation (made worse by deafness), everything almost.

—Henry Lawson, *Fragments of Autobiography*

Fight through ignorance, want, and care—
    Through the griefs that crush the spirit;
Push your way to a fortune fair,
    And the smiles of the world you'll merit.

—Henry Lawson, *The Uncultured Rhyme to His Cultured Critics*

Ode to Henry Lawson

Henry Lawson was a brave man.
As courageous as he has ever been,
the odds against him were so great!
His vainglorious stance against those odds
wasn't as deterrent as it should have been.
He stood his ground and lifted his spirits.
He kept his promise and trod up the road—
swag, bottle, and pen.

Henry Lawson was an angry man.
As ostentatious as he has ever been,
the odds against him were so great!
He stood his ground and lifted his spirits.
His exegetical scores against those odds
weren't as deterrent as they should have been.
He kept his promise and wrote what he saw—
swag, bottle, and pen.

Henry Lawson was a lonely man.
As misanthropic as he has ever been,
the odds against him were so great!
He stood his ground and lifted his spirits.
His euphuisms against those odds
weren't as deterrent as they should have been.
He kept his promise and fended his radical thoughts—
swag, bottle, and pen.

Henry Lawson was a deaf man.
As human as he has ever been,
the odds against him were so great!
He stood his ground and lifted his spirits.
His fury against those odds
wasn't so deterrent as it should have been.
He kept his promise and tramped along—
swag, bottle, and pen.

Henry Lawson

He was a man with driven eyes
that captured uttered words
with every phonetic detail,
drawn features of rawness
in shantytowns and sheeptowns.
His eyes tramped for undignified lives
characterizing heroics of survival
that were so written, so truly Australian.

He went afar from Sydney to Melbourne.
He tramped from Bourke to Hungerford.
He tramped from Hungerford to Bourke.
He tramped about the Darling.
He tramped with mates with his swag
to minimally rectify the sky-shorn raw.

In every shantytown, there were stories to tell or versify
of haggard mates who come from afar
        to freshen up and rejuvenate;
of lonely wives who make amends
        to keep their families under the roof;
of arrogant denizens who run the towns
        to make the place reasonably livable;
of ruddy drovers who herd sheep
        to the corrals to shear;
of himself he writes his yarns to earmark
        his loneliness with his driven eyes.

He frequented pubs to exorcise.
He drank to chase away demons.
He crawled in his cave to meander.
He wrote to epitomize yarns and verses,

whatever,
whenever
came to light,
whether sobriety
manifested.

There were always stories to tell or versify
when there were moments to spare without rancor,
whether with hearing mates or ladies.
He was always alone, nonetheless—
his true mate has always been his pen.

The Great Australian Rivalry

An embattlement sponsored—
two great Australian poets at their corners,
the sponsor shouted
above the fray—
punctuated rivals,
prodding to book the punches.

> *Did you hear no sweeter voices in the music of the bush*
> *Than the roar of trams and buses, and the war-whoop*
> *of the "push"?*
> *Did the magpies rouse your slumbers with their carol,*
> *sweet and strange?*
> *Did you hear the silver chiming of the bell-birds*
> *on the range?*[1]

Banjo lambasted Henry.

Aus-sie! Aus-sie! Aus-sie!
When you'd see them shouting,
you'd know they were rooting
for the homeland.

Aus-sie! Aus-sie! Aus-sie!
They were rooting for their heroes too.

Banjo came dancing in from his corner
plucking and strumming,
singing his scourging ballad,
bowing and kowtowing,
gloating in their vigorous chanting.
Ban-jo! Ban-jo! Ban-jo!
They were rooting for their hero,
you see.

---

[1]   Paterson, *In Defence of the Bush* (1892).

Kudos for the man who sang!
Kudos for the man who trotted!
Kudos for the man who heard
applauding accolades
languishing with the claque
as they chanted.
Ban-jo! Ban-jo! Ban-jo!
They were rooting for their hero,
you see.

> *You had better stick to Sydney and make merry*
> *with the "push",*
> *For the bush will never suit you, and you'll never*
> *suit the bush.*[2]

Henry recanted and licked his wounds.

Aus-sie! Aus-sie! Aus-sie!
When you'd see them shouting,
you'd know they were rooting
for the homeland.

Aus-sie! Aus-sie! Aus-sie!
They were rooting for their heroes too.

Hen-ry! Hen-ry! Hen-ry!

Henry with his cane in hand
a pipe clenched between his teeth
strode toward the center court
with a puzzling look,
bewildered—why the commotion?
Watching the crowning commotion,
the unequivocal chanting,
Hen-ry! Hen-ry! Hen-ry!
Clueless raving in the crowds,

---

[2]   Paterson, *In Defence of the Bush* (1892).

clueless waving from the crowds,
enthusiastically chanting,
Hen-ry! Hen-ry! Hen-ry!
Henry leaned on his cane
so utterly clueless—
Banjo chortled with a smirk.

> *Now in a shop in Sydney, near*
> *The Bottle on the Shelf,*
> *The tale is told – with trimmings – by*
> *The Jackaroo himself.*
> *'They made my life a hell,' he said;*
> *'They wouldn't let me be;*
> *They set the bully of the shed*
> *'To take it out of me.'*[3]

Henry retorted and slathered Banjo.

They were rooting for Henry, you see.
And that, he might have known.
But why? He agreed to do it.
He did what he had to do—
he had no clue
what was going on.
The claque isn't what he expected.

Unaware was he, but beware!
There was a catch lingering
without any priors for him—
an unpredicted predicated punch—
a stab in the back he couldn't fathom.

Yet all that envisaging commotion
forever fervently reverberating,
Hen-ry! Hen-ry! Hen-ry!
They were rooting for their hero, you see.

---

[3] Lawson, *Man from Waterloo* (1892).

Don't you see?
Henry just never smiled.
He never sang his own ballad.
Hen-ry! Hen-ry! They cried still.
What's this about?
They're singing a different song.
He sensed something stirring.

> *You've a down on 'trams and buses', or the 'roar' of 'em, you said,*
> *And the 'filthy, dirty attic', where you never toiled for bread.*
> *(And about that self-same attic—Lord! wherever have you been?*
> *For the struggling needlewoman mostly keeps her attic clean.)*
> *But you'll find it very jolly with the cuff-and-collar push,*
> *And the city seems to suit you, while you rave about the bush.* [4]

Henry fought back hard.

Hen-ry! Hen-ry! They screamed still.
He couldn't hear them calling
Hen-ry! Hen-ry! Hen-ry!
He just never knew why it was happening.
He wrote back his scathing verses though.
He knew something just wasn't right—
he just gave up and walked away.

Hen-ry! Hen-ry! Hen-ry!
They've been rooting for their hero still.

Henry rebukes:

> *And you think the bush is purer and that life is better there,*
> *But it doesn't seem to pay you like the 'squalid street and square'.*
> *Pray inform us, City Bushman, where you read, in prose or verse,*
> *Of the awful 'city urchin who would greet you with a curse'.* [5]

---

[4]   Lawson, *The City Bushman* (1892).
[5]   Lawson, *The City Bushman* (1892).

Curtis Robbins

Banjo for all his grandiosity
barely knew the rough
and confided it so,
unlike Henry
who knew the rough.

> *And the poets of the nation, singing-birds or carrion-birds,*
> *Bluff with cheap alliteration and the boom of empty words,*
> *Catch the crowd with cheating phrases, as a jingo laureate flings*
> *Recklessly his high defiance in the "grinning teeth of Things."*
> *They pretend to lead who follow this day's crowd with lying tact;*
> *Let them fling their high defiance in the stony face of Fact.*[6]

---

[6]   Lawson, "Nemesis" (1904)

The Sydney Monologue at the Henry Lawson Statue

Oh, Henry! Oh, Henry.
I am so utterly mesmerized
at the presence of your likeness
in black patinated bronze.

I see the bridge by the opera house
across the river from the garden—
it tings of Sydney's cultured artistry,
but your statue speaks of Australia's soul.

Light breezes sway multitudinous trees,
sumptuously tall and lanky variates
that beautify the greenery stumped
with sandstone walls and statues.

Wooden benches align winding walks
implanted along the hilly sprawl,
some taken by lovers and
some by tired strollers,

endless walks laid in Ss,
Js, and Us that ribbon along
on the swelling lawns
laden with mottled daydreams.

In your environs on top of the hill,
cars curb the streets;
joggers amble by at times
to impede my thoughts momentarily.

Curtis Robbins

It's a good thing, Henry! I'm
so intense and need to recollect.
My American mind has been tackling
accents of the Australian bush.

Cultural clashes make mishmash
out of literary mincemeat
laced with cacophonies
of acrimonious local color.

Words dance about the open page,
yet every syllable seem so hard to say,
trying to let our languished tunes
entertain those imperturbable ears!

I'm so sorry I am not attuned
to your shantytown songs of the bush—
I'm just so used to words that make mettle
out of being what you and I are.

It makes sense, Henry! For both of us—
it doesn't matter—the senselessness—
what matters is our impassioned voices
that sound so different to them.

Yet we are singing to them, Henry.
Our voices are tenors of our glories
I'm standing by you reciting the silent opus—
can you see how those words blossom?

Poet

Curtis Robbins was born in New York City in 1943. At the age of one, he lost his hearing while being treated for tonsillitis. He is a graduate of Gallaudet University, he attended NYU, and he received his doctorate from the University of Maryland in 1985. Currently, he is a retired adjunct associate professor, who taught—among other things—American Sign Language and Deaf culture for more than forty years prior to his retirement in 2007. Robbins has published several poems found in four anthologies: *No Walls of Stone* (1982), *The Deaf Way II Anthology* (2002), *Deaf American Poetry* (2009), and *Deaf Lit Extravaganza* (2013). His poem "In der Nacht" (In the Night) is found in two Holocaust anthologies: *Beyond Lament* (1998) and *Blood to Remember* (2002). Several other poems are found online, in several deaf and non-deaf publications, and in several textbooks on Deaf culture.

Printed in the United States
by Baker & Taylor Publisher Services